A PRIMER

I0437028

ON THE

SPATIAL DYNAMICS

OF

CRIME EMERGENCE

AND PERSISTENCE

By

Leslie W. Kennedy

Joel M. Caplan

Eric L. Piza

RUTGERS
Center on Public Security

2012

Newark

New Jersey

USA

Suggested Citation

Kennedy, Leslie W., Caplan, J. M. & Piza, E. L. (2012). *A Primer on the Spatial Dynamics of Crime Emergence and Persistence*. Newark, NJ: Rutgers Center on Public Security.

Produced by the Rutgers Center on Public Security

Based at Rutgers University's School of Criminal Justice, the Rutgers Center on Public Security (RCPS) offers a multidisciplinary approach to the academic study and practical application of ways in which democratic societies can effectively address crime, terrorism and other threats to public security. This involves the prevention of, protection from and response to natural or man-made events that could endanger the safety or security of people or property in a given area. RCPS engages in innovative data analysis and information dissemination, including the use of GIS, for strategic decision-making and tactical action. Visit www.rutgerscps.org

CONTENTS

PREFACE

There are many concepts, theories, technologies, and ideas that we rely on in the course of work as criminologists and crime analysts. This book summarizes how we understand them and how they relate to crime and illegal behavior at certain places. We can support all of the following statements with prior or ongoing empirical research, professional experiences, and expert practitioner knowledge. But, we do not bore you with the details here. Just ask us if you want to know more.

Respectfully,

The Authors

NATURAL AREAS

In 1942, Clifford Shaw and Harvey McKay published a model for the mapping of delinquency in urban areas that emphasized contextual factors. They identified "natural areas" from a series of map overlays for Chicago, Illinois to demonstrate that, over three decades, certain locations repeatedly experienced crime, despite the changing social characteristics of the people who lived there. This situational persistence resided, they said, due to the ways in which the important factors of criminogenisis converged at these areas. Shaw and McKay used this reasoning to document the areas in which crime would persist over time.

But, the narrative that they followed suggested a connection between bounded areas and behavior without actually being able to substantiate this link. Partly because of their reliance on census tracts and related data, Shaw and McKay were constrained in their assumptions about the links between social characteristics and crime. Also, the patterns that they expected, including a decrease in crime emanating from the inner city according to such things as concentric zones – a theory proposed by early ecologists Park, McKenzie, and Burgess in 1925, could not be demonstrated in research performed outside of Chicago. This made them susceptible to the criticism that underlying forces of competition and concentration were not being mapped through their analysis.

It has been more than 70 years since Shaw and McKay's original research emphasized contextual factors of crime. New advances in geographic information systems (GIS), micro-level data, and analysis methods provide an opportunity to overcome the limitations faced by them and others in their efforts to connect characteristics of communities with crime.

ROUTINE ACTIVITIES

Routine Activities theory (Cohen and Felson, 1979) states that crime is most likely to occur when there is a convergence of motivated offenders, suitable targets and a lack of capable guardians. This convergence typically occurs as a result of everyday patterns of activity across the life course. For example, the rise of residential burglary between the 1960's and 1970's was explained by a change in the routine activities of American households: The increased numbers of single-headed households and women in the workforce left homes empty and unguarded more often than had previously been the case. But, the presence of criminogenic environments heightens the chance of crime commission by offering motivated offenders highly vulnerable criminal targets. Contemporary research has shown that motivated offenders commit crime against suitable targets at certain places according to the environmental characteristics of those places that make it easier to complete the crime successfully and reap the rewards without punishment (e.g., getting caught).

Routine Activities theory is event focused. In order to apply the theory to practice, police need to focus on events that have not yet occurred by anticipating and controlling the behavior of individuals no matter where they are or where they are traveling to and from. This is a very difficult endeavor. What is more manageable for police agencies is to allocate resources to places that are most attractive to motivated offenders and to where crime is most likely to occur given certain characteristics of the environment. These are the places with the greatest risk and likelihood of crime. While many offenders may be responsible for a majority of crimes, very few places tend to account for most crime incident locations.

In the long-standing debate in criminology concerning what promotes crime, it is not enough to say that risk of crime increases when the numbers of criminals increase. What is more likely is that the risk of crime at places that have criminogenic attributes is higher than other places because these locations attract motivated offenders (or more likely concentrate them in close proximity) and are conducive to allowing certain events to occur. This is different from saying that crime concentrates at highly dense hotspots. It suggests, instead, that individuals at greater risk to commit crime will congregate at locations that are best suited for perpetrating it.

ENVIRONMENTAL BACKCLOTH

The 'environmental backcloth' refers to "elements that surround and are part of an individual and that may be influenced by or influence his or her criminal behavior" (Brantingham and Brantingham, 1981). Both the physical characteristics of places (e.g. buildings, public transportation stops, etc.) and the influence of such characteristics on the surrounding landscape based on individual cognitive assessments and routine activities contribute to the environmental backcloth. In other words, the environment is not merely a setting or a backdrop in which criminal and non-criminal behaviors occur, but rather a dynamic context comprised of the person-environment nexus involving interactional feedback loops and day-to-day situations, including both criminal and non-criminal activities.

The surrounding environment is very much a part of any criminal activity – as the environment emits cues which may or may not affect an offender's decision-making or daily routines. For example, crime attractors and generators will invariably impact how individuals view their environment, what signals they receive from it, and what type of behavior they believe they can participate in. Attractors are those specific things that attract offenders to places in order to commit crime. Generators refer to the greater opportunities for crime that emerge from increased volume of interaction occurring at these areas. Additionally, the presence of particular facilities can provide criminogenic opportunities. Other aspects like the demographic, economic, socio-cultural, legal and spatiotemporal characteristics of an area may also be considered. Most factors that comprise the environmental backcloth fit into three broad categories: (i) physical characteristics; (ii) demographic, socio-economic and cultural characteristics, and; (iii) person-environment characteristics.

PLACES AS UNITS OF CRIME ANALYSIS

Opportunities for crime are not equally distributed across places, or small micro units of analysis. Opportunity theorists have suggested that variations in crime are explained by opportunities to commit crime at locations that are accessible to the offender. This approach includes concepts of exposure, proximity, guardianship, and target attractiveness as variables that increase the risk of victimization. So, crime analysis and prevention activities should consider not only who is involved in the criminal events and where the crimes happened, but also the environmental characteristics of where crimes occur and cluster. A common thread among opportunity theorists and related scholarly thinkers is that the unit of analysis for "opportunity" is a place, and that the dynamic nature of that place constitutes opportunities for crime. A weaved landscape of micro places is an environmental backcloth.

Criminologists have traditionally utilized fairly large-scale areas, such as census tracts, as units of analysis in the study of crime. However, with time, and technological improvements, scholars have been able to incorporate smaller areas that more accurately reflect "micro-places," such as city blocks, street segments, and intersections, as units of analysis. It is also possible to model the landscape at an even smaller scale. Crimes could conceivably occur at any place in a jurisdiction. A victim who was robbed at 123 Main Street could just as likely been robbed at 115 Main Street if he stopped to tie his shoe, walked slower, or was delayed for any number of other reasons. To model such a continuous crime opportunity surface in a geographic information system (GIS), a grid of equally sized cells that comprise the entire jurisdiction could be used. Each cell represents a micro place throughout the landscape. The cell size should be selected as a function of street segment/block lengths. For example, half the mean block length in the jurisdiction might guide the choice of cell size. In this way, an environmental backcloth is constructed in a manner that reflects the unique landscape of each jurisdiction and its street network (on which people often travel and to which crime incidents are often geocoded). This micro cellular grid method is consistent with expectations about the continuous nature of criminogenic risk.

As an attribute of places, opportunity for crime is not an absolute value, a dichotomous variable, or a static quotient. It is rarely or never zero. Opportunity varies in degrees and changes over space and time as public perceptions about environments evolve; as new crimes occur; as police intervene; or as motivated offenders and suitable targets travel. Assessing spatial opportunities for crime requires a conceptual framework that is attuned to incorporating multiple dynamic factors and producing intelligence that serves strategic decision-making and tactical action. This can be achieved through risk assessment.

RISK ASSESSMENT

Risk assessment is defined as "a consideration of the probabilities of particular outcomes" (Kennedy and Van Brunschot, 2009). High or low risk is often attributed to conventional offender-based risk assessments, first established many decades ago when researchers began to demonstrate that certain characteristics of offenders were correlated with their subsequent behavior. Offender characteristics are scored and combined to form a scale that is indicative of "risk"—such as the risk of re-arrest or reconviction, the risk of absconding while on bail, or the risk of violating conditions of parole or probation.

Turning attention away from the offender and on to the place where crime occurs, the attractiveness of risk-based approaches to crime control and prevention is that risk assessment can tie information closely to both strategic and tactical decision-making. It provides a means by which decision-makers can evaluate success of interventions and plot future actions. It comports with the idea that the public has anxieties about crimes that translate into demands for prevention strategies to reduce victimization risk. And, it addresses the idea that certain places can be more dangerous than others and, therefore, demand greater police attention. Risk assessment can articulate evaluation plans used to determine the effectiveness of interventions and the efficacy of certain types of resource allocation decisions. In these ways, risk assessment can be an attractive framework for policing that takes advantage of new information and intelligence, while involving a more aware and sophisticated police force directly in a dialogue with the public about safety and security issues.

The concept of risk is not new or unique to the criminal justice community, and risk assessment has a long history of being used to identify, prevent or control crime. Risk models provide tools for identifying hazards and vulnerabilities that can lead to crime outcomes. Risk provides a metric that can help tie different parts of the crime problem together and offers a probabilistic interpretation to crime analysis that allows us to suggest that certain things are likely to happen and other things can be prevented based on our risk assessments. When "opportunity for crime" is thought of in terms of "risk of crime," places can be evaluated in terms of varying degrees of criminogenic risk relative to certain nearby or far away features of the landscape.

SPATIAL INFLUENCE

Spatial influence refers to the way in which features affect places throughout a landscape. Criminogenic features have historically been modeled in a geographic map in ways that are contrary to how people experience and conceptualize their environments. When assessing the risk of crime to occur at conceivably any location throughout a city, the use of finite objects in a geographic information system (GIS) are poor representations of criminogenic features, as they bear no particular relationship to the dynamic environments of which they are a part. Points, lines, and polygons that define objects on a map are approximations of features of landscapes, but have no theoretical or empirical link to their geographies. The way people (e.g., motivated offenders and suitable victims) conceptualize and operate in space is an important consideration for the mapping and assessment of crime risk throughout landscapes. Cartographically modeling these conceptualizations and the spatial influences of crime factors in a GIS in a way that reflects the actors' views can yield more meaningful and actionable information for use by public safety professionals.

Operationalizing the spatial influence of a crime factor tells a story, so to speak, about how that feature of the landscape affects behaviors and attracts or enables crime occurrence at places nearby to and far away from the feature itself. When certain motivated offenders interact with suitable targets, the risk of crime and victimization conceivably increases. But, when motivated offenders interact with suitable targets at certain places, the risk of criminal victimization is even higher. Similarly, when certain motivated offenders interact with suitable targets at places that are not conducive to crime, the risk of victimization is lowered. Geographic information systems can produce maps that visually articulate these environmental contexts where certain crimes are more or less likely to occur as a result of the combined influences of one or more crime factors affecting the same place. In this way, criminal behavior is modeled as less deterministic and more a function of a dynamic interaction that occurs at specified places.

But understanding these crime-prone places requires more than just a snapshot of how offenders and victims interact at a point in space. The best way to map crime factors for the articulation of criminogenic "backcloths" is to operationalize the spatial influence of each factor throughout a common landscape rather than a-theoretically mapping the factors as points, lines or polygons in a manner that keeps them disconnected from their broader social and environmental contexts. To succeed at this task, we need to incorporate information about places that we would expect to increase risks of crime.

Decades of criminological research have identified a variety of independent variables that are significantly correlated with a variety of crime outcomes that can be used to inform our expectations. For example, an empirical study of gang-related shootings operationalized the spatial influence of known gang members' residences as "areas with greater concentrations of gang members residing will increase the risk of those places having shootings" and depicted this as a density map created in a GIS from known addresses of gang members' residences. It should be noted, though, that spatial influences of crime factors may differ at certain days of the week and times of the day. So, be sure to consider the possible temporality of spatial influences of factors for different crime types and in different settings.

Thinking about crime correlates not as finite objects but rather as centers of radiating criminogenic influence across a landscape enables the cartographic modeling of environments in terms of micro-level place-based risks that are more enduring than just the characteristics of the people who frequent these areas. This approach is consistent with ideas that were popular among ecologists, repeated by environmental criminologists when talking about "environmental backcloths", expressed in the key elements of problem-oriented policing, and now appear in terms of risk terrain modeling.

If we return to the theme of spatial analysis that propelled Shaw and McKay in their studies of delinquency, we can argue that missing in their analysis was an accounting for 'spatial influence' as a way of operationalizing the contextual effects of location on crime. Using modern day computing technology, we can take this operationalization and demonstrate how locations can be defined by the spatial influence of key factors that connect to crime. Using this diagnostic and cartographic technique, we can take a step beyond the Shaw and McKay approach and forecast the emergence and persistence of crime based on the vulnerability portrayed by the spatial influences of particular features of landscapes. This approach (as demonstrated in the next few chapters) permits the study of spatial concentration of crime using evidence-based methods – building on the insights of ecologists, but using tools and data that permit the study of the micro-level components of these places in ways that suggest meaningful interaction between place-based features and illegal behavior.

PRESENCE OR ABSENCE OF FEATURES

The following map shows the locations of shooting incidents (the crime) and bars, clubs, fast food restaurants and liquor stores (the crime risk factors) in Irvington, NJ. These features of the environment are correlated with shootings in many empirical research studies, both in Irvington and other settings. Looking at the map, shooting incidents appear near these features. But, only one shooting incident was at the exact same address as one of them.

[Map on Next Page]

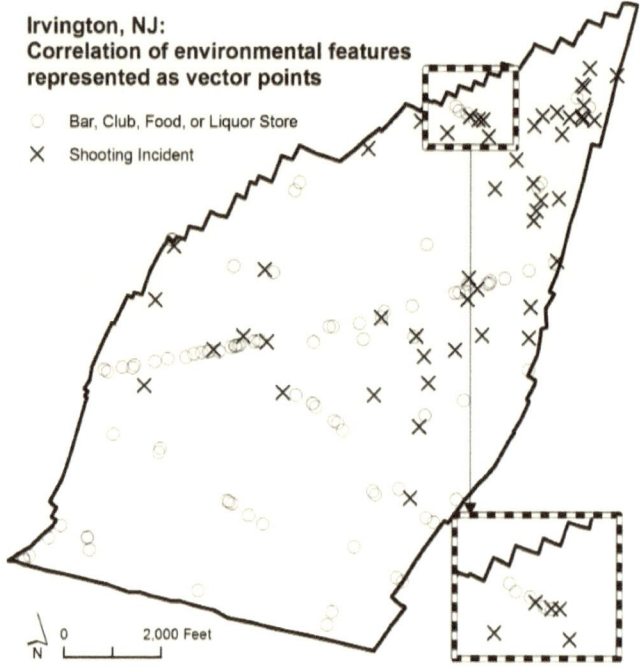

Irvington, NJ:
Correlation of environmental features
represented as vector points

○   Bar, Club, Food, or Liquor Store

✕   Shooting Incident

0   2,000 Feet

N

CONCENTRATION OF FEATURES

As shown in the following map, the spatial influence of bars, clubs, fast food restaurants and liquor stores is related to their concentration, or density, at places throughout the municipality. This density map is symbolized according to standard deviational breaks, with all places colored in grey as being in the top third of the most densely populated. These high density places hosted 20 out of 58 (34%) shootings during 2007. "Places" are defined in the raster grid as cells sized 100ft—which is about 1/3 of a block length.

[Map on Next Page]

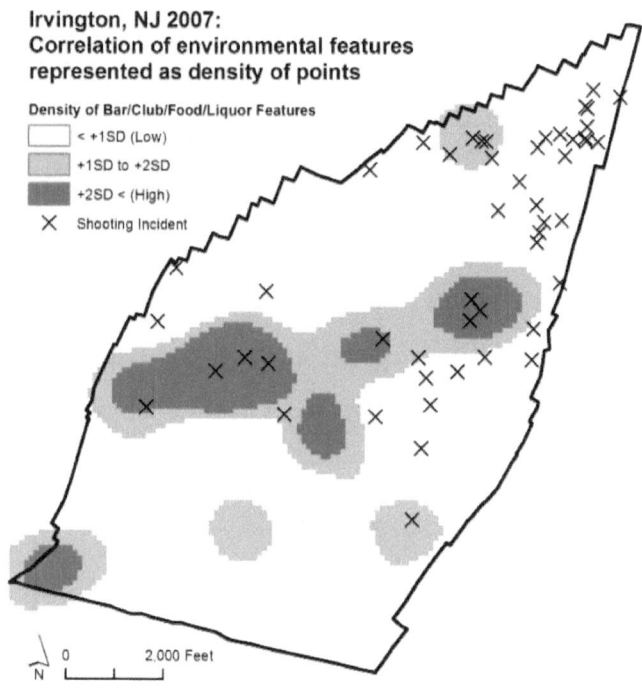

Irvington, NJ 2007:
Correlation of environmental features
represented as density of points

Density of Bar/Club/Food/Liquor Features

☐ < +1SD (Low)

▨ +1SD to +2SD

▧ +2SD < (High)

✕ Shooting Incident

0   2,000 Feet

N

SPATIAL DISTANCE

Perhaps bars, clubs, fast food restaurants and liquor stores are the venues where most suitable victims hang out or where the most likely and motivated offenders visit, become intoxicated, or lose self-control. But, due to increased police presence or other capable guardians such as bouncers, witnesses or CCTV cameras, offenders do not shoot their victims inside or directly outside of such facilities, but are more likely to wait until they are a certain distance away. Thought of in this way, spatial influence could be a function of distance from the closest feature.

As shown in this map, 31 shootings (or 53% of all incidents) occurred within one block from bars, clubs, fast food restaurants or liquor stores. This result could arguably be due to identifying a larger catchment area to which shootings are aggregated. However, the coverage area of places with high density values is 0.8 square miles, and the coverage area of places within one block is 0.7 square miles. So, more shootings occurred in a smaller area that was deemed affected by nearby criminogenic features in a conceptually meaningful way.

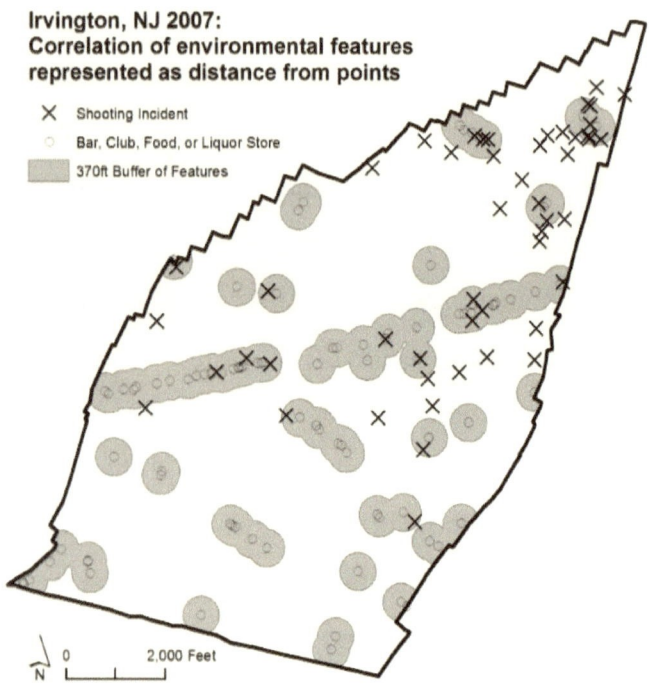

Irvington, NJ 2007:
Correlation of environmental features
represented as distance from points

✕ Shooting Incident

○ Bar, Club, Food, or Liquor Store

▨ 370ft Buffer of Features

0   2,000 Feet

N

HOTSPOTS:
CRIMES CLUSTER AT SPECIFIC LOCATIONS

Hotspots are clusters of crime at the same general area. These are important as research has shown that up to 50% of crime is produced by 3% of city locations (Sherman, Gartin, and Buerger, 1989). However, hotspots are often defined by locations where crimes already occurred, without any consideration of their timing. In fact, crimes occur sequentially in time. So, hotspot maps can be a bit deceiving because they only show the spatial (not temporal) part of a crime clustering phenomenon. This issue has been referred to as the "stationarity fallacy", which emphasizes the fact that crime maps often display combinations of unrelated incidents that occurred over time and are plotted in hotspots as though they are somehow connected beyond sharing a common geography.

From a crime control and prevention perspective, crime hotspots are really just symptoms of other phenomena at places. A sole focus on crime hotspots is like observing that children frequently play at the same place every day and then calling that place a hotspot for children playing, but without acknowledging the presence of swings, slides and open fields. These features of the place (i.e. suggestive of a playground) attract children there instead of other locations absent such entertaining features. Hotspots of crime, then, serve more as a proxy measure of places where the dynamic interactions of underlying criminogenic factors exist or persist over time. Spatial influences of crime correlates at micro places affect and enable the seriousness and longevity of crime problems and hotspots. Crime suppression efforts can be targeted at hotspots. But for crime prevention, it is best to identify and focus on certain social and environmental factors and try to effectively mitigate them.

NEAR REPEATS:
CRIMES CLUSTER AT SPECIFIC TIMES

Near repeat, or contagion, models assume that if a crime occurs at a location, the chances of a new future crime occurring nearby increases for a particular period of time. As a consequence, many near repeat incidents over time could result in crime hotspots. Examinations of near repeats explain how past crime incidents can serve as predictors of new crime occurrence at certain times. But, near repeat analysis must be done in hindsight (with past data), so (by itself) it is not practical for prospective policing operations. However, it gives practitioners a certain level of statistical confidence that new crimes could happen within a certain distance of past crimes and within a certain period of time from the prior incident.

Some places may contain characteristics that make them more likely to promote crime than other, less suitable, areas. This attraction would likely be based on a number of factors. If we consider the past experience with crime as an isolated indicator of future victimization, this would parallel crime analysis approaches based on event dependence, such as hotspots. As an extension of, or companion to, hotspot analysis, near repeat analysis explains how past crime incidents can serve as predictors of new crime incidence. Bowers and Johnson (2004) discussed two views of near repeats. The first argues that repeat victimization results from a contagion-like process. For example, after the first burglary, the risk of another crime is boosted. This occurs as offenders will return to take advantage of the good opportunities in this target. In contrast, a second explanation suggests that victimization will recur based on a time-stable variation in risk or "flag".

In the studies that have been done to-date, researchers have found evidence to support the near repeat phenomenon in a variety of crime types and settings. Investigations of near repeats provide an important extension of hotspot analysis as they account for the temporal link between crime events and do not just assume that behavior that takes place in close proximity at whatever time in a set frame (e.g., a month, a year) has anything to do with other behavior located nearby.

RISK TERRAIN MODELING

Risk terrain modeling (RTM) is a spatial analysis technique that facilitates the examination of multiple datasets that share geography as a common denominator (Caplan and Kennedy, 2010). It 'paints a picture' onto a map of crime events that are statistically likely to occur at places with similar conditions. Individual crime (risk) factors are important, such as those owned by motivated offenders or potential victims, but the co-location of certain features (and their spatial influences) are especially important in assessing crime-prone places. Many places abound daily with motivated offenders, suitable victims, and no capable guardians. But crimes do not always occur there. Why? Because these elements must simultaneously exist at enabling places to yield criminal events.

Risk terrain modeling articulates the environmental backcloth for crime by layering spatial influences of multiple crime risk factors. Now, qualities of places themselves do not create crime. They simply point to locations where, if the conditions are right, the risk of crime or victimization will be high. RTM assumes a step that is basic to the development of geographic information systems in assuming that certain locations can acquire attributes that, when combined in prescribed ways, create contexts in which certain outcomes are made more likely. As suggested above, the attributes of open space, presence of children, and proximity to schools may indicate a playground. These attributes combined can be used to anticipate the types of behavior that would be expected in a playground—reducing the uncertainty that forecasts about what would transpire there are wrong. In this way, RTM uses the spatial influence of environmental features as a means of assigning likelihood (or risk) that certain events will happen at particular places. Outcomes may be benign (e.g. children playing) or they may take on a more sinister character where a combination of certain types of factors related to crime creates a context in which events can occur.

Risk defines the likelihood of an event occurring given what is known about the correlates of that event, and it can be quantified with positive, negative, low or high values. Using environmental risk as a metric to describe criminogenic places, it is possible to model how crime emerges spatially and temporally. Modeling broadly refers to the abstraction of the real world at certain places. Specifically within the context of risk terrain modeling, modeling refers to the act of attributing the presence, absence, or intensity of qualities of the real world to micro-places throughout a landscape to represent the likelihood of crime occurring there. Risk terrain modeling produces a metric for place-based opportunity, as measured by the spatial influences of place-based (crime) risk factors.

VISUALIZING RISK TERRAINS

The co-location of spatial influences of certain crime factors or features of a landscape are used to assess crime-prone places, and to build risk terrain models and maps.

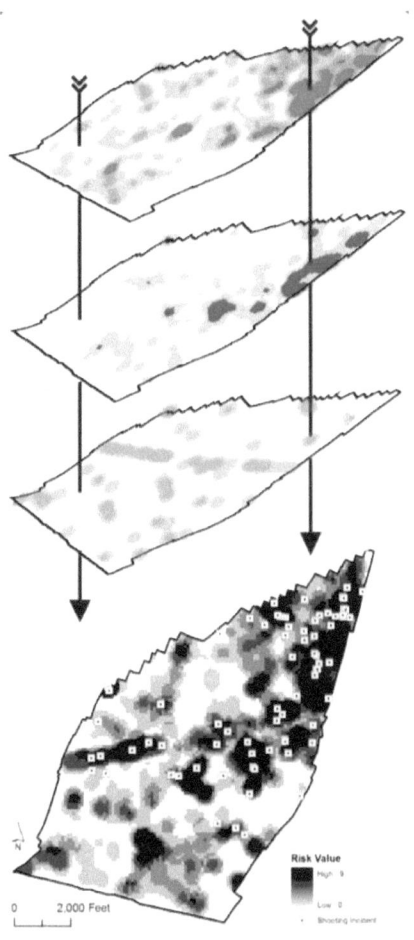

Vulnerability and Exposure

Places and environments have characteristics that encourage or discourage the occurrence of crime and, therefore, raise or lower criminogenic risk. Assigning risk levels to certain features of environments requires that we understand (i.e., through past research and experiences) their relative importance in attracting or supporting crime. The risk posed by each criminogenic feature is located at one or more places on a landscape; their confluence at the same place contributes to a risk value that, when raised a set amount, increases the likelihood of crime. This risk value – a measure of the clustering of the risk factors, can be used to forecast where crime will occur and (possibly) cluster over a period of time. Risk values derived from risk terrain models are a measure of vulnerability to crime.

People can live in vulnerable areas defined by an agreed upon set of criminogenic features and their spatial influences. In the absence of motivated offenders, the existent risk of crime may be relatively low. So, risk of crime is a function of vulnerability within the context of other factors that carry different weights relative to one another. Crime risks, then, are both place-based and situational – affected by exposure to individual events that appear from location-to-location, and by exposure to places where events cluster over time (i.e., implying contagion). The concept of exposure defines risk as a spatial-temporal function of previous crime events. Cartographically modeling vulnerability as the clustering of risk factors (i.e., risk terrain modeling), and then interpreting vulnerability in the context of exposure, permits a strategy to identify, monitor and control these environments.

Of course, the connection between criminogenic features and crime depends on one's ability to operationalize risk emanating from such features to all places throughout the landscape. Recall that the concept of spatial influence refers to the way in which features of a landscape affect places throughout the landscape. It is based on the idea that everything relates to everything else, but things that are closer are more related. If this is true (both in terms of promoting or discouraging certain types of behavior), then the cumulative effects of spatial influence should be such that certain places within the spatial influence of many criminogenic features should be more vulnerable to crime than places that are not influenced by one or more criminogenic features. Defining vulnerable places, then, is a function of the combined spatial influence of criminogenic features throughout a landscape that contribute to crime by attracting and concentration illegal behavior. Risk terrain modeling creates this metric for measuring and communicating vulnerable places.

JOINT UTILITY OF NEAR REPEATS
AND RISK TERRAINS

Analyzing risk terrains along with event-dependent assessments is useful for generating a more complete understanding of crime problems because environmental backcloths are present before, during, and after instigator or near repeat incidents. Such environmental contexts may influence whether a person or property is targeted. While the immediate area surrounding an instigator incident may have heightened levels of risk *post factum*, such an area may already have been at high levels of risk in the first place. In fact, research suggests that instigator and near repeat crime events occur at places of higher risk in comparison to non-instigator/non-near repeat incidents. Further, instigator and near repeat pairings are influenced by similar levels of place-based risk.

As illustrated below, crimes that cannot be prevented and that serve as instigator incidents (for near repeats) are most likely to attract near repeat incidents at nearby places of high environmental risk—as opposed to micro-level places within the expected near repeat bandwidth that have very low risk. Stated another way, instigator crime incidents may create a "pie" of a certain radius within which near repeat incidents are most likely to happen during a certain timeframe. But within this pie, some "slices" are more likely to have crimes than other slices due, in part, to the underlying risk terrain.

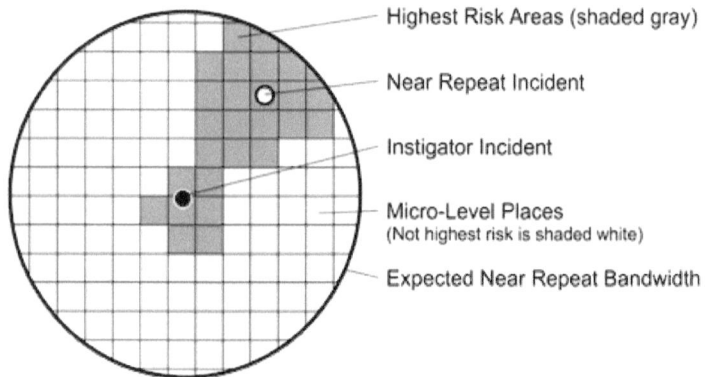

Instigator incident and near repeat incident within the expected near repeat spatial bandwidth on a risk terrain surface.

One advantage of knowing that a near repeat phenomenon exists for crimes in a jurisdiction and that crimes are more likely to occur at high risk places is the ability to prioritize each new crime incident according to its propensity for being the instigator event for near repeat crimes. Assuming that every new crime incident is a potential instigator for near repeats, priority can be given to new crimes that occur at high risk places with other high risk places in close proximity. Place-based risk assessment with RTM permits real-time evaluation of the propensity for a new crime to become an instigator for near repeats.

Imagine, for instance, a crime analyst plotting a new crime incident on a risk terrain map (shown in the following map with an x'd circle). She then draws a buffer around it equal to the expected near repeat bandwidth to isolate all the micro places within the buffer. Then she identifies all the places within the buffer that pass the high-risk threshold, such as all places with risk values >=3. Now she can advise police commanders about the proportion of high-risk places within the buffer: in this case, 87 out of 237 = 37%. This can inform decisions about whether to allocate limited resources to that crime's buffer area given the opportune places within it for near repeat crimes. Extra-spatial factors, such as knowledge about potential victims or offenders could also be considered. This resource allocation decision could be made in consideration of all other recent crime incidents that occurred so that priority can be given to those areas with the greatest propensity for near repeat crimes within the expected timeframe.

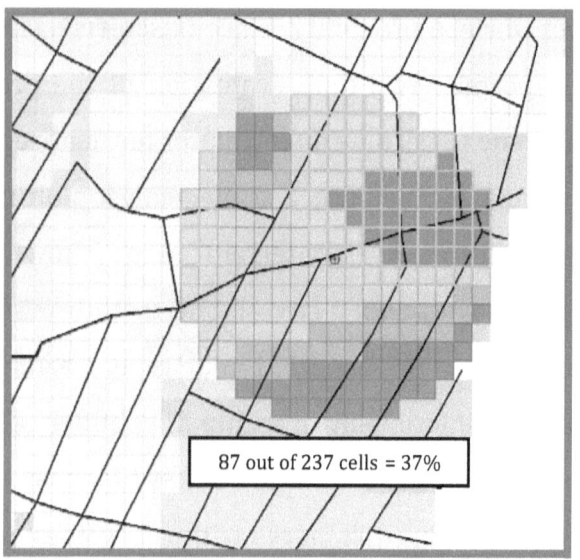

87 out of 237 cells = 37%

INTEGRATING SPATIAL ANALYSIS TECHNIQUES FOR CRIME ANALYSIS AND RESPONSE

Risk terrain modeling methods provide police with a means to communicate criminogenic risk and to work proactively to protect against features of the landscape that attract or enable crime. Problem-oriented policing (POP) has become a common practice within police agencies, but leading criminologists argue that the contemporary use of POP rarely adheres to the "S.A.R.A." model that POP is built upon. Many efforts can be classified as "shallow problem solving" whereby police officers conduct superficial analyses of problems and resort to traditional law enforcement tactics (e.g. arrests, stop-and-frisks, knock-and-talks, serving warrants) rather than incorporate a more holistic approach that directly addresses the underlying problems. This may be partly related to the analytical products commonly used in the creation of police initiatives. Hotspot maps, for instance, show the concentration of crime but offer little in the sense of context. By articulating the environmental context of crime incident locations, risk terrain modeling helps to identify and prioritize specific areas and features of the landscape that should be addressed by a targeted intervention.

The joint utility of risk terrain modeling, hotspot mapping and near repeat analysis offers police a unique opportunity to suppress crimes immediately by allocating resources to existing hotspots. They can, in addition, seek to prevent crimes through interventions at places that are most attractive to motivated offenders given certain characteristics of the environment, even if crimes are not yet occurring there. Empirical research has repeatedly demonstrated that including a measure of environmental risk yields a better model of future crime locations compared to predictions made with past crime incidents alone. Such findings confirm that crimes tend to occur at places with higher environmental risks, especially if crimes occurred there already.

HOLISTIC APPROACH TO
CRIME DETECTION AND PREDICTION

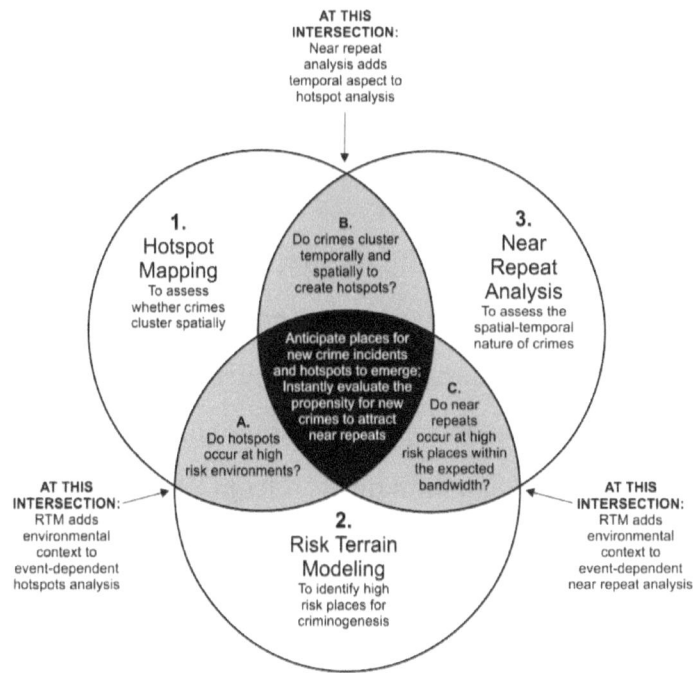

The first step of a holistic approach to understanding crime (#1 in the figure, above) is hotspot analysis to assess whether (and where) crimes cluster spatially in the jurisdiction. The second step (#2 in the figure) is to model environmental risks with risk terrain modeling to identify high-risk places for criminogenesis.

The joint utility of information derived from Steps 1 and 2 (A in the figure) is to determine if crime hotspots occur at high risk places or within high-risk clusters. This knowledge can help to explain the underlying environmental risk factors that may attract and generate hotspots. The third step (#3 in the figure) is near repeat analysis to assess the spatial-temporal nature of past crimes. The joint utility of information derived from Steps 1 and 3 (B in the figure) is to help explain the event-dependent and temporal nature of crime hotspots in the jurisdiction. If a near repeat phenomenon exists, then the joint utility of information derived from Steps 2 and 3 (C in the figure) is to evaluate the propensity for new crime incidents to become instigators for near repeats based upon the proportion of high-risk places within the expected near repeat bandwidth.

The culmination of all three steps is information products that can inform short- and long-term strategic planning and at least three tactical deployment decisions. Information product **A** enables police to respond immediately to places where crimes cluster and crime problems persist, and to respond preemptively to high-risk places. Information product **B** gives police a temporal window for which near repeat crimes are most likely to follow new crime events. This knowledge can help to reduce the costs of deploying extra resources for long or uncertain lengths of time following new crime incidents. This, in turn, can help to reduce alert fatigue among patrol officers who are assigned to patrol places nearby to new crime incidents. Information product **C** allows police to prioritize place-based deployments of resources by comparing new crime incidents relative to all others according to the surrounding environment's suitability for hosting new near repeat incidents. Priority can be given— and limited resources (re)allocated, to new crime incidents that have more high-risk "slices of the pie" than other incident locations.

KEEPING THE ANALYST IN CRIME ANALYSIS

The development of new crime analysis techniques tends to imply that older methods are outdated and, therefore, no longer useful. Sometimes this initiates and encourages the adoption of much needed new methods for crime analysis. Other times, it discourages innovative approaches to crime analysis because of the uncertainty among practitioners as to what is actually the "best" and, then, which old approach to doing things the new approach should replace.

In contrast to a competitive view over which analytical technique or technology outperforms the other, the combined utility of event-dependent approaches to crime analysis, such as hotspot mapping and near repeat analysis, and environmental approaches, such as risk terrain modeling, offer an advanced toolbox for law enforcement information production. The best analytical tool is a skilled (human) operator who knows how and when to apply each crime analysis method, and then what to do with the resultant information products.

Theory of Risky Places

Given the current thinking about crime vulnerability based on concentrations and spatial influences of features and events, we offer an analytical strategy to model risky places that combines the conceptual insights of crime emergence and persistence, advances in geospatial analytical techniques, and micro-level data. This framework supports three propositions:

1. All places are risky, but because of the spatial influence of criminogenic features, some places are riskier than others;

2. Crime emerges at places when there is high vulnerability based on the combined spatial influences of criminogenic features at said places; and,

3. The overall effect of risky places on crime is a function of differential vulnerability and exposure throughout the landscape.

These propositions provide a basis for analyzing the processes whereby crime emerges, persists, or disappears. In the long-standing debate in criminology concerning what promotes crime, it is not enough to say that risk of crime increases when the absolute numbers of crime incidents increase throughout a jurisdiction. What is more likely is that the risk of crime at places that have certain criminogenic attributes is higher than other places because these locations attract motivated offenders and are conducive to allowing crime events to occur. Strategies to address crime problems, therefore, must incorporate both the spatial and temporal patterns of recent known crime incidents and the environmental risks of micro places if they are to yield the most efficient and actionable information for police resource allocation.

CRIME EMERGENCE, PERSISTENCE, AND DESISTANCE

The risk that comes from increased vulnerability tied to features in the environment, and exposure that derives from recent past crime incidents, concentrates at places and influences new crime patterns that occur there. The Theory of Risky Places framework permits the study of spatial concentrations of crime using evidence-based methods, building on the insights of the ecologists but using tools and data that permit the study of the micro-level components of these places in ways that suggest meaningful interaction between place-based features and human behavior. We do not rely on the knowledge of the physical or social characteristics of individuals who enter and leave these locations, only on the geographic factors that make these places risky.

When crime disappears from vulnerable places, should these places still be considered unsafe or suitable areas for crime to occur again? The answer based on prior empirical research is yes. Vulnerability does not change unless one or more factors that comprise an environmental backcloth (i.e., as articulated by a risk terrain model) are mitigated. The spatial-temporal context for crime is merely exacerbated when vulnerable places are exposed to recent past crime incidents.

Risky places are formed as a result of the confluence of the spatial influence of certain factors combined with conditions of exposure. Crime forecasts using this analytical approach can be replicated using off-the shelf GIS software and existing datasets and resources. It is not enough to assume that the risk of crime at micro places increases because crimes already happened there, or because there was an absolute increase in crime counts throughout a macro area. What is more likely is that risk of crime increases at places with certain qualities that attract motivated offenders and are conducive for crime events to occur. Crime analysis and forecasting, therefore, must incorporate spatial vulnerabilities and exposures at micro places if it is to yield the most efficient and actionable information for police resource allocation and intervention planning.

RISK REDUCTION STRATEGIES

Spatial influence can be stronger closer to known criminogenic features and weaker farther away. This effect is not a constant, but one that can be mitigated through programs that reduce risk. Acknowledging that research is correct in pointing to spatial influence as a key factor in crime emergence, it is sensible to consider a crime reduction strategy that focuses on mitigating the influences of certain factors on crime. If spatial influence increases the chance of crime and its patterns over time, it should be equally the case that reducing spatial influence should reduce the incidence of crime.

Risk reduction strategies directed at spatial influence involve a number of approaches. These include strategies that focus on the characteristics of locations, mobilizing the people who live and frequent these areas to protect themselves and their surroundings; strategies that increase the situational prevention of areas that block opportunities for crime, including target hardening and surveillance; strategies that work to improve the conditions in areas that might breed criminal activity, including the influence that comes from crime attractors and generators; and strategies that target previous crimes and offenders. Each of these approaches involves risk reduction considered in terms of spatial influence.

PLACE-BASED POLICING

Spatial crime analysis inevitably leads to strategies that direct law enforcement to particular locations, and they often use the tool most directly available to them to solve problems: arrest. While we do not suggest replacing this as an intervention strategy, the Theory of Risky Places provides a complementary approach that focuses attention on the ways in which places matter in crime events. It is important to consider risk reduction that comes from addressing the collective spatial influences of certain factors in creating vulnerability and increased exposure to crime as an equally important approach to crime control and prevention.

Since crimes cluster spatially, crime control and prevention resources should be similarly concentrated to achieve maximum impact. This ideal has become well established in law enforcement, with contemporary police agencies directing resources to high crime places. Place-based policing practices have consistently demonstrated their effectiveness. They offer a more efficient method of policing than offender-based strategies. But, crime suppression and prevention efforts at these places cannot succeed outside of an understanding of the combined effects of the social and physical environments in which the offender operates.

Resilient crime hotspots are both a function of the presence of motivated offenders as well as the attractive and/or generative qualities of the environment that serve as cues to offenders that certain places are suitable to commit crimes. Offenders occupy space and bring to certain locations characteristics that might threaten others and disrupt social interaction at these locations. They may also engage in illegal activities (such as, gangs or drugs) that themselves change the risk character of these locations (and also attract attention from law enforcement). Most often a crime analyst's measure of the presence of offenders is designated as the number of crime incidents reported or arrests that are made and tabulated by police in crime reports. But, there are other types of measures to use that are more enduring than the crime incident. Tying predictions of crime to geographic places and their characteristics provides the basis for connecting attributes of space to actual behavior that occurs at these places, such as high frequencies of crimes (i.e., hotspots) or near repeat victimizations. It also takes the police beyond a tactical response to crime occurrence to one that is more strategic, anticipating where resources will be needed to respond and prevent newly emerging crime problems.

RISK-BASED CRIME INTERVENTION

In 1995, Reboussin, Warren, and Hazelwood described a map that displays the spatial orientation of only a single phenomenon (e.g. crime) as a "mapless map." As explained by Rengert and Lockwood in 2009, "A mapless map is a mere description since it describes how one variable is distributed in space; whether it clustered or uniformly distributed for example. In order to determine "why" it is distributed the way it is, the spatial distribution of at least one other variable needs to be considered" (109). By articulating the environmental context of crime incidents and hotspot areas, risk terrain modeling could help police identify and prioritize specific features of the landscape to be addressed by an intervention.

Risk-based interventions should include at least three simultaneous activities—at least one that relates to each of the following categories:

1. Reducing the criminogenic spatial influence of one or more environmental crime risk factors.

2. Evidence-based practices, such as activities related to target-hardening, situational prevention, and/or community awareness.

3. Using policing activities/patrols to deter and incapacitate known/motivated offenders.

The intervention can be unique to a jurisdiction and does not need to be complex, time consuming, or expensive. Design the intervention in a way that does not place an undue burden on police department resources or finances. This means that the intervention's activities should be considered to be "reasonably" sustainable/repeatable under "normal conditions" without external (i.e., grant) funding.

Intervention activities should focus on mitigating risks posed by both offenders and the environment. Crime hotspots are both a function of the presence of motivated offenders as well as the attractive and/or generative qualities of the environment that serve as cues to offenders that certain places are suitable to commit crimes. Further research is needed to determine which element of crime events must come first; that is, a suitable environment or motivated offenders who commit multiple crimes to form hotspots. At the point in time when interventions are often called for, however, both of these elements likely exist and, therefore, must be mitigated simultaneously.

Crime intervention activities should be consistent with the idea that target areas may be (environmentally) resilient places for criminogenesis. Intervention activities should be implemented and sustained for a long enough period of time to suppress the frequency of targeted crimes to the point that hotspots are no longer "hot" and thus no longer perceived by motivated offenders as "tried-and-true" spots for repeat crimes. Activities must focus on mitigating spatial vulnerabilities and exposures, and be sustained for as long as the risky environment is resilient.

PLACE-BASED EVALUATIONS

Sherman and Eck argued in 2002 that evaluations of crime-prevention programs should include measures of "exactly what police do—and when they do it" because it allows researchers to "tell the difference between programs that 'do not work,' and programs that simply 'did not happen'" (p. 302). Measures of enforcement activity can add perspective as to how program effects were achieved with successful interventions. Therefore, evaluations should begin with a descriptive analysis to include a variety of success measures, including the number of arrests and other street-level enforcement actions (e.g. record checks) made by the officers, the number of weapons and narcotics seized, and other enforcement-activity data. Particularly in the context of violent crimes, which run a high risk of serious injury or death, these types of figures that are publically reported by police agencies following an intervention are viewed by many stakeholders as meaningful and significant dividends.

An outcome analysis should compare the targeted micro areas with equivalent control micro areas. For instance, control areas could be selected through a propensity score matching (PSM) process to ensure that treatments and controls are balanced on covariates of interest. A pre/post crime count analysis at the macro and micro levels should be conducted to measure the effect of the intervention. At the macro-level, counts of crimes that occurred within all target areas (and control areas, respectively) should be empirically tested for significant changes between the pre- and post-intervention time periods.

A micro level count analysis can more directly address the micro place-based nature of intervention activities and to assess the impact of interventions without results being confounded by aggregation effects coming from the ecological fallacy. The ecological fallacy refers to an error in the interpretation of results whereby assumptions about the intervention's success or failure are based solely upon aggregate statistics for the macro target areas. To state that every micro-level place within the larger target area did or did not have a reduction in crime based upon aggregate data may not be accurate. Rather, local variations in crime concentrations and, presumably, criminogenic characteristics of these locales can differentially impact the ability of the intervention to deter crimes. Evaluate whether any significant changes between pre- and post-intervention crime counts aggregated to macro target areas are generally realized across all micro places within the target areas.

It is difficult to know with certainty if crimes are displaced outside of the target areas because it is nearly impossible to associate the occurrence of new crime incidents with the absence of where they would have occurred otherwise. So, rather than conclude that displacement or diffusion happened based solely on results of "traditional" displacement/diffusion tests (e.g., weighted displacement quotient), the spatial nature of crimes in each jurisdiction, pre- and post-intervention should be assessed. To clarify, overall crime counts may significantly decrease within the target areas post-intervention. However, evaluations should seek to determine whether the locations of new crimes occurred at similar or different places compared to before the intervention. For example, if pre-intervention hotspot places remain frequent hosts to incidents of crimes post-intervention, then it suggests that the spatial nature of crimes post-intervention is generally consistent with pre-intervention patterns.

This type of assessment process could be used to improve on the ways in which police both design interventions and assess their effectiveness. A spatial analysis of the micro place effects of the intervention on crime incident locations is particularly important for maximizing the scope and validity of evaluations about location-specific (i.e., targeted) interventions by police. Further, analytical methods that consider the impact of targeted police interventions while controlling for environmental risk factors beyond crimes themselves can serve as diagnostic tools to help interpret why the intervention produced a certain outcome.

COMMENCING SPATIAL ANALYSIS

Incorporating a holistic approach to crime analysis and resource deployment necessitates "buy in" from agency leadership. This commitment must be institutionalized in a manner that ensures that executives and those under their command incorporate the approach into daily operations. This could be established and reinforced through existing law enforcement management strategies, such as CompStat, which can be leveraged to ensure that commanders put commensurate effort towards mitigating the underlying problems that generate crime. In addition, the "S.A.R.A" model of problem-oriented policing could be embraced in a manner that encourages commanders to devise plans that directly address the factors identified in a risk terrain model. Notably, the use of spatial risk analysis techniques will be highly dependent upon the availability of data.

It is likely that dynamic characteristics of criminogenic features can further identify risk heterogeneity. A housing complex experiencing a sharp increase in narcotics-related calls-for-service, for example, may be more criminogenic (at that moment in time) than complexes where reported narcotics activity is stable. Identifying common attributes linking the crime incidents comprising a hotspot may also be beneficial. For example, identifying a crime series—a "run of similar crimes committed by the same individual(s) against one or various victims or targets" – can help police anticipate crime emergence when an incident with a similar modus operandi occurs outside of the existing hotspot.

Modern GIS technology supports the real-time updating of data through the linking of mapping software and large databases that primarily contain information on crime, calls-for-service, and officer activity. If a police department collects, stores, and updates risk factor data in an ad-hoc manner (as opposed to the systematic collection of crime data), it may be challenging for the agency to routinely incorporate spatial risk-based crime analysis into its operations. However, the recent uses of risk terrain modeling in various settings suggests that police departments are able to access and incorporate risk data into their analytical framework.

APPENDIX

GIS: A geographic information system (GIS) is a computer software application for managing, editing, analyzing and displaying data which are spatially referenced to the Earth. Spatial data can be represented as individual layers, displayed as separate entities, or be combined with other layers to be displayed together. Imagine a GIS as a high-tech overhead projector from the "old days" that used transparent plastic sheets and dry-erase markers as inputs that were then projected on a wall. If you think of each transparent sheet as a separate map layer, and you place all of the transparent sheets (map layers) on top of each other, you can see through all of them at-once. In this way, you can see relationships among the data that overlap in certain areas. Essentially, GIS does this digitally and in much more sophisticated ways.

VECTOR AND RASTER DATA: Vector is the most common GIS data type used in the social sciences. It uses points, lines, and polygons to represent map features. Vector data are excellent for representing discrete objects such as incident locations, streets, or administrative boundaries. But the vector format is not as good for representing things that vary continuously over space, such as temperature, elevation, or crime risk.

Raster data use grids made up of equally-sized cells to represent spatially continuous data. Each cell is assigned real world coordinates and one attribute value (such as risk). The user defines the cell size, allowing for very fine or course raster surfaces. Even when the cell size is very small, you can see the individual square cells when you zoom in. Raster grids cells are like pixels on a TV or computer screen.

Whereas vector map layers are oriented toward the depiction and analysis of discrete objects in space (represented as points, lines, or polygons), raster grids are oriented more toward the qualities of space itself.

RASTER CALCULATOR: Raster map layers can be added, subtracted, multiplied, divided and queried using map algebra and the Raster Calculator tool in Esri's ArcGIS. Map algebra is a general set of conventions, capabilities, and techniques that have been widely adopted for use with a GIS. The Raster Calculator creates a new grid on which the value of each cell is computed by applying map algebra and/or logical functions to the value of the cell on one or more existing grids. Essentially, it produces a new composite map. Consider, for example, the two raster (grid) layers shown in the figure below. In each layer, cell values range from 0 to 1. If Raster Calculator were to be used to add each cell's values on these two grids, the result would be a composite raster map with cell values (potentially) ranging from 0 to 2.

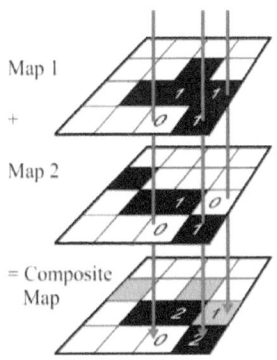

Selecting Buffer and Bandwidth Distances When Operationalizing Spatial Influence: Certain features of a landscape can attract or enable certain types of crimes beyond their immediate surroundings. Empirical research suggests that this "spatial influence" of features extends no more than just a couple of (urban) street blocks. So, the length of a radius for spatial influence around environmental risk factors should be selected as a function of the average (or median) length of block faces in the jurisdiction. It should be no more than 2 or 3 times that distance. For example, if the blocks in Springfield are about 500ft, then a reasonable radius around bars could be 250, 500 or 1,000 feet. For a (real) example, here is a link to a 3-page report demonstrating the risk of crime posed by proximity to vacant properties in Philadelphia, PA: http://www.rutgerscps.org/docs/KensingtonProject_VacantParcelShootingRisk_Report.pdf

In general, we recommend that you calculate (or if need be, estimate) the length of street blocks in your study setting and then set buffer or bandwidth to be a multiple of that. The final decision is somewhat subjective, but 1 to 2 block lengths is reasonably justified. Do not use distances greater than 4 blocks.

BIBLIOGRAPHY AND RECOMMENDED READINGS

Bowers, K. J. & Johnson, S. D. (2004). Who commits near repeats? A test of the boost explanation. *Western Criminology Review, 5*(3), 12-24.

Bowers, K.J., & Johnson, S.D. (2005). "Domestic burglary repeats and space-time clusters: the dimensions of risk." European Journal of Criminology, 2(1), 67-92.

Brantingham, P. J., & P.L. Brantingham. (1981). *Environmental Criminology*. Beverly Hills, CA: Sage.

Caplan, J. M. & Kennedy, L. W. (2010). *Risk Terrain Modeling Manual: Theoretical Framework and Technical Steps of Spatial Risk Assessment*. Available from Rutgers Center on Public Security, Newark, NJ at www.riskterrainmodeling.com

Caplan, J. M. & Kennedy, L. W. (Eds.) (2011). *Risk Terrain Modeling Compendium*. Available from Rutgers Center on Public Security, Newark, NJ at www.riskterrainmodeling.com

Caplan, J. M. (2011). Mapping the spatial influence of crime correlates: A comparison of operationalization schemes and implications for crime analysis and criminal justice practice. *Cityscape, 13*(3), 57-83.

Caplan, J. M., Kennedy, L. W., & Baughman, J. (in press). Kansas City's Violent Crime Initiative: A Place-Based Evaluation of Location-Specific Intervention Activities during a Fixed Time Period. *Crime Mapping*.

Caplan, J. M., Kennedy, L. W., & Miller, J. (2011). Risk terrain modeling: Brokering criminological theory and GIS methods for crime forecasting. *Justice Quarterly, 28*(2), 360-381. [2010, online first]

Caplan, J. M., Kennedy, L. W., & Piza, E. L. (in press). Joint utility of event-dependent and environmental crime analysis techniques for violent crime forecasting. *Crime and Delinquency*.

Caplan, J. M., Moreto, W. D., & Kennedy, L. W. (2011). Forecasting Global Maritime Piracy Utilizing the Risk Terrain Modeling (RTM) Approach to Spatial Risk Assessment. In L. W. Kennedy and E. F. McGarrell (Eds.), *Crime and Terrorism Risk: Studies in Criminology and Criminal Justice*. New York: Routledge.

Cohen, L. E. & Felson, M. (1979). Social change and crime rate trends: A routine activity approach. *American Sociological Review, 44*, 588-608.

Kennedy, L. W. & Van Brunschot, E. (2009). The Risk in Crime. N.Y.: Rowman and Littlefield.

Kennedy, L. W. & Caplan, J. M. (2011). Risk Terrains and Crime Emergence. In J. McGloin, C. Sullivan, and L. W. Kennedy. *When Crime Appears: The Role of Crime Emergence*. NY: Taylor & Francis.

Kennedy, L. W., Caplan, J. M., & Piza, E. (2011). Risk clusters, hotspots, and spatial intelligence: Risk Terrain Modeling as an Algorithm for Police Resource Allocation Strategies. *Journal of Quantitative Criminology, 27*(3), 339-362. [2010, online first]

Kennedy, L. W., Yasemin Gaziarofoglu, & Caplan, J. M. (2012). *Global Risk Terrain Modeling Manual: Theoretical Framework and Technical Steps of Worldwide Spatial Risk Assessment.* Available from Rutgers Center on Public Security, Newark, NJ at www.riskterrainmodeling.com

Park, R., McKenzie, R., & Burgess, E. (1925). The City:Suggestions for the Study of Human Nature in the Urban Environment. Chicago: University of Chicago Press.

Reboussin, R., Warren, J., & Hazelwood, R. (1995). Mapless mapping in analyzing the spatial distribution of serial rapes. In Block, C., Dabdoub, M., and Fregley, S. (eds.), *Crime analysis through computer mapping,* 69-74. Washington, D.C.: Police Executive Research Forum.

Rengert, G. & Lockwood, B. (2009). Geographical units of analysis and the analysis of crime. In Weisburd, D., Bernasco, W. and Bruinsma, G. (eds.), *Putting Crime in its Place: Units of Analysis in Geographic Criminology,* New York: Springer.

Rusnak, D., Kennedy, L. W., Eldivan, I. S., & Caplan, J. M. (2012). Countering the Threat of Terrorism: Applying Risk Terrain Modeling in Turkish Cities. In C. Lum and L. Kennedy (Eds.), *Evidence-Based Counterterrorism Policy.* New York: Springer-Verlag.

Shaw, C. & McKay, H. (1969). *Juvenile Delinquency and Urban Areas.* Chicago: University of Chicago Press.

Sherman, L. & Eck, J. E. (2002). Policing for Prevention. In Lawrence W. Sherman, David Farrington, and Brandon Welsh, eds. Evidence-Based Crime Prevention. New York: Routledge.

Sherman, L. W, Gartin, P. R., & Buerger, M. E. (1989). "Hot Spots of Predatory Crime: Routine Activities and the Criminology of Place." *Criminology 27*, 27-55.

www.ingramcontent.com/pod-product-compliance
Lightning Source LLC
Chambersburg PA
CBHW020335290526
45785CB00005B/2028